Many

flies

have

feathers

Ivor Cutler

Trigram Press London

Acknowledgements are due to the editors and producers
of the following journals and programmes in which
some of these poems first appeared: A I R London,
Ambit, Aquarius, B B C, The New Statesman,
Oyster, Pentameters, Transatlantic Review, 20th Century,
Writers Workshop

Designed printed and published by Trigram Press
15 Southwark Street London SE1
Printed in England

Many flies
have
feathers.

9

Not
many flies
have
feathers.

10

My Mother Has
Two Red Lips

My mum has
two red lips.
So has two cherries.
And a limp
when she
breaks a bone.

She walks
a mile
on a sunny day
with a baggy parcel
of nuts.

11

If I wish you
To arrive
I sit facing the
Canvases and
Do not concentrate
On your arrival.
When you arrive,
I shall smile
Lightly, too embarrassed
To rush,
Also considerate for
You and touch your
Arm or hand or
Finger to let you
Know I am glad
Then retreat to a
Quiet room where
We can talk eye
To naked eye.

12

Big mice
have
big teeth.

13

I am painted
on the
inside canvas
of my tent.
Enter
and find me
all round you
loving you.

14

I like sitting.
The best
thing about sitting
is
sitting down.
When you are young
they say,
"sit up!"
That is
stupid.
You can not
sit up unless
your spine is
funny.
I sat up, and
bent.

They forget
they were
young.

A pupa lay
In a soft wooden bed
Yellow and milky
In a pale brown setting.
Her teeth were
Tough as dessicated
Coconut.
On her rudimentary
Hand lay a splinter
Which her benevolent
Old mum left behind
As a weapon to fight
Her way to the exit,
Like a cinema-goer
Who has just seen a
Tough film.
"I do hope I am going
Out", thought the pupa
Fighting into the
Centre of the tree.

16

Today
absentmindedly
I laid a Granny Smith.

It was
sold
as
a extra-large egg.

2/3d for 6.

The lady took it back.
This is a Granny Smith.
It is a extra-large egg
he said look at the marks.

She boiled it.

Then she took it back again.

a walnut
great tidings.
join a black
grape to a
green grape.
seaweed.

18

The arrival
of
a biscuit-tin
in our family is
an event.
We gather round
in ones and twos
(sometimes threes)
to observe.
Red wrappings
rustle to the floor
in
an intense silence.
"Oh"s and "Ah"s
follow
the removal of the lid
and
mouths full of crisp biscuit
saunter casually
back to the card room,
lips
curved in an
unnatural smile.

19

A Love Poem

I ate a brick
To mortify myself.
A London brick,
Soft and mellow.
The large chewy
Grains scraped
Flakes of yellow
Enamel down
My throat, cutting
At my tonsils
When the salivary
Flow
Was low.
Mortified, I
Turned to a staple
Diet, but the quiet
Call of yellow brick
Sounded its tocsin
And I was forever
Lost to conventional
Nourishment.

20

If everybody
liked everybody,
there would
be nobody left
for anybody
else.

Country Idyll

The fleet crawls through the sludge.
It towers above the meadow grass.
Mallows and sedge are bruised
By the bulk of its hulk
As it thwarts the canal bowel.

A rating stands at ease.

An admiral admires a dead dace,
Floating in effluent,
Bleak red pinhead eyes,
Pale belly up.
Puzzled peasants scratch their scalps
With firm straws.
A toad slides a film
Across its horny eye.
The flagship navigator searches torn logs
For a precedent.
As he raises his arm for a stretch,
The wool vest at his armpit
Creaks in the balmy saltless air,
And a lark in the sky catches a sweaty whiff
As she tweets her faultless ditty and poops
A tiny poop down a frigate's funnel.

In the evening,

In the evening,
A concertina is brought on to deck
And a grizzled salt squeezes windy
Slow hornpipes through its flaccid brass
Reeds edged with green pretty verdigris.
Solemn bearded sailors
Go through the motions,
Vault mercilessly about
Over careless junior ratings.
A temporary salt-lick is erected
By the grog barrel,
To stifle mutiny.

At 4 bells,
A deputation hot from the fo'c'sle
Hoists a signal on the mizzen:
WE ARE LOST.
There is a stunned silence,
Then every sailor in the fleet
Vaults the gunwale
On to lush bottom grass,
Spits on his palms,
Hoists his duffel and ambles into the dark,
Making for—who knows:
Home,
Port,

23

The village pub,
An amiable scrubber.

On board,
The navigator cries on to his chart;
The admiral sits with empty eyes
And separated knees.

Whilst
waiting for my accountant
to
receive me
I
weighed the daffodil
I
had
brought him
on the letter balance.
5/16ths of an oz!
5/16ths of green and yellow beauty.
I did not know a flower had weight
before.

When
next
I hold her in my arms
I shall think,
7 stone 9
and she,
11 stone 12.

For sixpence
I whisper,
"You are beautiful."
For a shilling
I whisper,
"You are beautiful,
despite
certain unfortunate features."
For a florin
I call
"What an
interesting physiognomy
you possess."
For five bob,
"You are
exceedingly ugly."
For ten,
"Ech!"
And,
for a quid,
"I love you!"

Look at them laugh!
It is women,
giggling at men.
But their faces
are flat.
Men do not know
they are a show.
'See my muscles!'
'See how bowled over
you are
by
my clever seduction technique!'
'This is how the
eternal combustion engine works!'

And
inside,
she is giggling,
and
bored.

27

A little boy, pee—
ring
over
the edge of a table,
sees
a dice with 5 dots.

He
does not
know
that at the other
side
it says
2 dots.

Phonic Poem

A car
can go
fast on
a hill
with no
brakes
and oil
on the
hub.
It can
not stop
so it
has a
spill.
Mum and
Dad get
a cut.
See Bill
bleed.
Bleed Bill bleed.
Kate do
not cry.

If you
do
Ann will

29

be sad
to see
it
and Ted
will fret.
Phil,
run to
the phone
for a
nurse
to make
us well.

I see
Nurse.
Nurse make
us well.
We are
ill from
a spill
on the
road as
we took a
spin.
Dad has
a cut

on his
lip.
It hit
the wheel
as he
drove fast.
Mum cut
her cheek.
See how
it shines.
Bill is dead.
He lost
his blood
in the
crash.
Kate, Ann
and Ted
are sad
for Bill.
He was
their
chum.
Phil will
walk
us home

31

a-
long
the pave-
ment to
our
house
29
Redb-
urn Avenue.

To Giorgio Morandi

A chair.
And a table.
A man sits,
elbows on the table.
An eye in his head.
In the wall,
a window.
He sees
through the window.
His foot,
in a shoe,
rests on the floor.
A bird flits by.
The white wall
is matt.
Its texture
irritates the man
as he tries
in vain
to empty his head
to let a fresh thought
fill it.
As his teeth meet
they make a soft click,
like pebbles
in the water.

I
used
to lie in bed
with women I loved
and
have sex.
With this
woman
I
lie in bed
and
have love.
Whatever
we do
is love,
even sex.

34

dear mum a
little bird flew on the pane
its claws
scrabble for a
foothold and flecks
of shiny yellow
flutter down
on to the sill
i
cannot reach the window
to let it in but
by drawing it
in my new drawing book
and holding it for him to see
i think
i am encouraging him
to persevere
i have only been sick twice
today and the doctor
thinks
ive a fair
chance

35

If all the corn-
flakes in the
world were floated
from New York
in an easterly direction
and all the
sugar in Cuba
were floated
north-east
and if all the
evaporated milk in Europe
were pushed west
and
all the children in the World
thrown into the
Atlantic

"Old Iron Man!"
They call. I
Bristle with strong
Delight and run
Upstairs to the
Kitchen
Mirror.
Patting my skin to
Shake off old
Epithelium,
I dance an ancient
Ballroom step in
Shrunken undies
To the tune of
The one o'clock
News.
Patting cologne into
My armpits, I totter
Down the stairs
Into the street,
Leaving the door ajar.

The Purposeful Culinary Implements

Open,
You patent-leather canteen!
Lift your
Fresh-cheeked faces,
Electro-plated nickle silver cutlery!
Run twinkling to the
Damask tablecover
And lay down flat
Into a pattern
To stimulate
My salivaries.
Complement the chinaware,
The fresh sausage rolls,
Crisply succulent,
The roundels of boiled beetroot
Each a crimson chariot-wheel
Fit to speed Mars,
The God of War.
Green lettuce leaves
Stroked with white
With,
Coyly esconced in their troughs,
Boiled shrimps,
Pink as cherubs.

38

O knives
Forks
And spoons!
Fulfil yourselves.
Then lay
In the washing-up bowl,
To emerge
Radiant
And be set
By a soft loving hand
Back in your
Patent-leather canteen
To sleep
And drowsily wait
Another purposeful waking.

It is brown under
Here sighed the lady
Who lifts grass.
Sam raised himself
With a slow elbow and
Pulled her down by him.
See here, he smiled,
Unbuttoning her
Silly blue blouse with
Wise old fingers, it
Stands to reason.
Look at that sun,
He pointed, unflicking
Her bra and resting
Her grateful breast
In his warm cupped
Palm.
I see, she gulped quietly
And lay back.

40

Has enemy
noticed
that tunnels
are thinner
than they
used to be?

They dig
thick tunnels.
Soon
they are
thin tunnels.

Nobody knows
where
the thick
goes.

41

I found
my son
in the
lavatory
having intercourse
with a meningococcus.
"What's wrong
with your sister,
son?" I muttered
and turned
away embarrassed.
Yet proud.
No one
in our family
had
ever done it
to a germ
before.

Had
I forgotten
during the war
men
comforting themselves
quietly
and sadly

in the desert
with sandflies;
sometimes whole handfuls.
But
they wore
a proud look too:
the look of men
keeping
themselves clean
for
their wives
and
sweethearts.

"Carry on,
Son,"
I
muttered through
my tears,
patting his wings.

On One Hand

On one hand

my Dad

is sad.

On the other

I can see

the hard work

gladden his heart.

He bends

in a field.

His braces are tense.

He sweats.

The smell of work

catches my nose

as I approach.

"Hello, Dad.

Here's your bread.

Here's your wine.

Crouch and eat."

I wish I were dead.
My senses are so fine
it is agony to be conscious.
Even a thrush over a tree.
Even a cool wind on my forearm.

I am in love.
Is this my punishment?
God, must I pay for every damn thing?

Yes, Ivor, you are growing.
You can not grow without pain.

It will stop when I'm grown?

Hm hm hm hm!—
Or when you give up.

45

A bird
flies
in the sky,
wings
along its body.
Its beak
kisses
the wind.

Once upon a time
There were 500 naked men
Who had a religion called
Love God.
One day they decided to show
God that they loved Him
By making a loud kissing sound.
They would arise simultaneously
From their black polyvinyl
couches at a prearranged signal.
This was made by an atheist
Slamming his fist into a plank
Of 8 by 1 deal.
He did it.
So they rose simultaneously,
Making a loud kissing sound.
God heard it.
It brought him to his feet,
Surprised but pleased.
As a reward,
He made them
Parthenogenic.
But they were
So embarrassed
That nothing
Ever came of it.

47

My sock
is
round my foot.
My sock
is
in my shoe.

How can it
not only be
in two places
but 2 shapes?

Socks
are more cunning
than
they let on.

48

Red birds
fly
in my blood.
They
roost
over the wrist
and
make it swell.
Doctor Pote
can not
check my pulse.
I feed them rape
and hemp
to hear
their bubbly song
through my pores,
fine as vermicelli.
Put your ear
to a bulge
and listen
through a pore:
it is so fine.

49

There and Back—
Via Sweden

A nun runs
on a string.

A fly clings
to a kite.

A hen
laves its feet.

Milk quietly
turns to cheese.

Milk turns
quietly to cheese.

My cock
lays an egg.

Spiders eat
their young.

A monk jumps
up on a bush.

The even keel
Of your soft moods.
I touched a moth's wing
It pulled free
Leaving a wing. Here
Moth, return and get
Your left wing,
It lies betwixt my
Finger. Get stuffed
She retorted
Civilly enough
For a monowinged moth
I just learned to fly
Straight
So keep my wing
To dust the shelf
Of your memories
And flew
In the fire
With a siss.

51

A
lemon
on the grass
is
sour.
But your sweet face
is like
the inside
of
a dark grape.

52

I reap
what I sow.
Others
sow in my field.
I reap
that too.
This is the miracle
and
excitement of life.
The faces
of
those in whose fields
I
sow
are
worth
hanging about
to watch.

My father once
had intercourse
with a polar bear
in Canada.

If
you ask him
he will deny this,
not completely astonished.
"Canada?"
he will shout
in
a restrained manner,
playing
for time.

54

When I
entered Heaven,
I slipped
on the floor
and
had to
apologise.

A still, small fly
Sits
Poised on a
Smooth white
Pill.
He hums
Old melodies
Heard at Mum's
Bony breast
As he lapped the
Juicy hot
Milk.
Mum was certified
TT.

Derek, -the fly-
With a wicked
Smile
Dashes into the
Air,
Zooms
Over Hymie Goldfish
In his bowl
and—P O W !
Drops a busy
On to the surface.

56

Hymie doesn't care,
He is extremely
Busy himself
Thanking God
He took spherical
Trig. as a child.

Derek doesn't
Know that Hymie
Doesn't care.
He didn't
Take Yiddish
For his 'O' Levels.

U.K.

Two balls
ran down
a hill.
One landed
on its side,
the other
upside down.

U.S.A.

Two fried eggs
ran down
a hill.
One landed
sunny side up,
the other
over easy.

58

I Can See Abie's Neck

I can see
Abie's neck
As he lies
Snoring on the earth.
Black flies
Walk about
His bald head.
His knee
Glints by the fire.
The white sky
Is a pure sheet
To cover his hurt.

You can see
The main road
If you lift
Your head,
And peer
Over the blood.

bless the
mediaeval woodman
and the mediaeval
cabinetmaker
piecing
warm and moist wood
into a useful box

A mountain of
Grey fluffy eggs
Rolled along the
Valley, loading
The winey air
With spores.
Many dreamers
Screamed
Others climbed.
Only a few
Relaxed,
And lay on top
Smiling at the
Sun.
"This is great"
Shouted Jed,
Stretching his
Gnarled legs and
Easing his
Hips.

61

A horde of flies
with black feathers
landed silently
in winter
and
ate the crop.